Hummingbirds

Tracy C. Read

FIREFLY BOOKS

A FIREFLY BOOK

Published by Firefly Books Ltd. 2017
Copyright © 2017 Firefly Books Ltd.
Text copyright © 2017 Tracy C. Read

For Charlotte

First printing

Publisher Cataloging-in-Publication Data (U.S.)
Names: Read, Tracy C., author.
Title: Exploring the World of Hummingbirds / Tracy C. Read.
Description: Richmond Hill, Ontario, Canada : Firefly Books, 2017. | Series: Exploring the world of --- | Includes index. | Summary: "Up-close images and fascinating facts about hummingbirds" – Provided by publisher.
Identifiers: ISBN 978-1-77085-946-3 (hardcover) | 978-1-77085-947-0 (paperback)
Subjects: LCSH: Hummingbirds – Juvenile literature.
Classification: LCC QL696.A558R433 | DDC 598.764 – dc23

Library and Archives Canada Cataloguing in Publication
Read, Tracy C., author.
    Exploring the world of hummingbirds / Tracy C. Read.
Includes index.
ISBN 978-1-77085-946-3 (hardcover).--ISBN 978-1-77085-947-0 (softcover)
    1. Hummingbirds--Juvenile literature. I. Title.
QL696.A558R43 2017   j598.7'64   C2017-902464-7

Published in the United States by
Firefly Books (U.S.) Inc.,
P.O. Box 1338, Ellicott Station, Buffalo, New York 14205

Published in Canada by
Firefly Books Ltd.
50 Staples Avenue, Unit 1, Richmond Hill, Ontario L4B 0A7

Cover and interior design: Janice McLean/Bookmakers Press Inc.

Printed in China

 We acknowledge the financial support of the Government of Canada.

Front cover:
© Dennis W Donohue/Shutterstock

Back cover:
© Martin Mecnarowski/Shutterstock

Back cover, inset, left:
© Seaphotoart/Shutterstock

Back cover, inset, right top:
© mbolina/Shutterstock

Back cover, inset, right bottom:
© Ondrej Prosicky/Shutterstock

CONTENTS

FLYING MACHINES

Only the hummingbird is designed to hover in place in midair, flapping its wings up to 200 beats per second to feed at a flower.

MEET THE HUMMINGBIRDS

It's a little like seeing a shooting star—did it really happen? The hyperactive hummingbird buzzes in and out of sight so quickly that the experience of spotting one of these creatures hovering at a flower is sometimes over before it registers in our human brain.

Recent fossil evidence proves that some 32 million years ago, an early hummingbird once made its home in Europe. Today, the more than 340 hummingbird species—all evolved to hover and drink flower nectar for sustenance—live only in the New World.

The world's smallest birds got their start in South America's lowlands, eventually forging new territories in the shadow of the Andes Mountains. In Colombia, Ecuador and Peru, they carved out exclusive neighborhoods in a range of habitats, from valleys to mountain peaks. They ultimately conquered the tropical forests, shrublands and savannas of northeastern South America, Central America, Mexico and the West Indies.

In much of North America, we don't have a chance to enjoy some of the more dazzling species first-hand—the coquettes, emeralds, brilliants and mountain-gems. Even so, the brave hummers that venture north of the Rio Grande display all the intriguing physical and behavioral traits of the other members of their big family.

Let's find out how the tiny, adaptive hummingbirds manage to succeed in a competitive world.

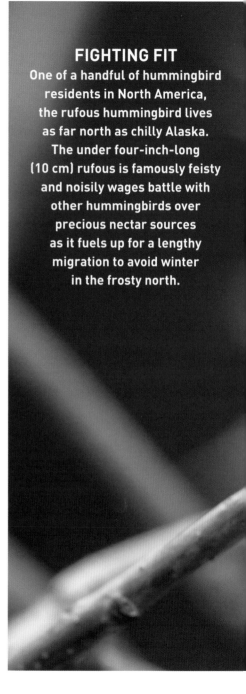

LAID-BACK LOOK-ALIKE
The Allen's hummingbird is easily confused for the rufous but has a less combative approach to life, perhaps because of the appealing climate of its California territory. Thanks to the nice weather, stay-at-home females might reproduce up to four times a year.

Hummingbirds range in size from the diminutive bee hummingbird, a mere 2³⁄₈ inches (6 cm) long and weighing up to two grams, to the giant hummingbird, which can top out at 8¾ inches (22 cm) and 20 grams. This selection of hummers illustrates several sizes and characteristics.

Green-crowned Woodnymph
Panama, Colombia, Ecuador, Peru
3¹⁄₈–4³⁄₈ in (8–11 cm); 3–4.5 g

Violet-tailed Sylph
Colombia, Ecuador
3¾–8¼ in (9.5–21 cm); 4.5–5 g

White-tailed Hillstar
Colombia, Ecuador, Peru
5¹⁄₈–5½ in (13–14 cm); 8.5–9 g

Chestnut-breasted Coronet
Southeast Colombia, Ecuador, Peru
4½–4¾ in (11.5–12 cm); 7–7.5 g

Booted Racket-tail
Colombia, Ecuador, Peru, Bolivia
3–5⁷⁄₈ in (7.5–15 cm); 2.5–3 g

Frilled Coquette
Central and eastern Brazil
2¾–3⅛ in (7–8 cm); 2–3 g

Scaly-breasted Hummingbird
Central America; Colombia
4½–5⅛ in (11.5–13 cm); 8–10 g

Great Sapphirewing
Colombia, Ecuador, Peru, Bolivia
6¼–7⅞ in (16–20 cm); 9–11 g

Golden-tailed Sapphire
Northwestern
South America
3¾–3⅞ in
(9.5–10 cm);
4.5 g

Snowcap
Central America
2⅜ –2½ in
(6–6.5 cm);
2.5 g

Chemical pigments in the feather barbules produce the hummer's noniridescent colors. The glittering iridescent colors are structural, the result of the angle of available light that hits microscopic air sacs in the barbules on the top third of the feathers.

ANATOMY LESSON

How does a high-performance lifestyle affect the design of the hummingbird, one of nature's smallest warm-blooded creatures?

Boasting over 900 feathers, more per square inch than any other bird, the hummingbird is supported by a skeleton of lightweight, porous bones. Powerful chest muscles conceal a mighty heart, capable of pumping up to 1,250 beats per minute in flight. Its efficient lungs absorb some 250 breaths each minute, transferring oxygen to its bloodstream and preventing its body from overheating.

Unlike any other bird, this aerial acrobat hovers in place to feed, using a specially adapted bill to access the nectar and sweeping its rigid wings in figure eights some 50 to 80 times per second. It can fly forward, backward and up and down as well. By rotating its wings nearly 180 degrees around its highly flexible shoulder joints, it is able to achieve lift with both forward and backward strokes.

The hummingbird meets the needs of its high metabolism by feeding regularly through the day. High-energy nectar is quickly digested and processed, with energy stored in the liver as fat for future use. On cold nights, the hummer enters a state of torpor by lowering its temperature and halving the energy it needs to survive each day.

Last, but not least, the hummer exploits its big brain, developing and retaining a mental map of its previous feeding locations.

SMALL WONDERS

Weighing under two grams, the bee hummingbird, top left, also known as zunzuncito, is the smallest bird in the world. A broad-tailed hummer, middle left, holds the record for longevity, at 12 years. Bottom left, the desert-loving Costa's avoids the heat by dining at dusk.

LOW-KEY APPROACH

Defying the colorful presentation of so many hummingbirds, this brown violetear goes about its business dressed in muted, drab tones. But in the right light, its bright blue-green throat patch glimmers. This hummer likes to hawk for flying insects in forest canopies from Guatemala to Bolivia and from Venezuela to Brazil.

Found in Mexico, the western United States and western Canada, the rufous hummingbird, seen here, has set the record for the longest hummingbird migration, flying at least 3,500 miles (5,600 km) between Alaska and Florida.

Cruise control
A hummingbird might hit speeds of 60 miles per hour (100 km/h) during a courtship display but typically flies at 25 to 30 miles per hour (40–48 km/h).

Wings
A hummer's arm bones are shortened and its hand bones lengthened so that the wing is mostly hand.

Off the clock
A hummingbird works hard to gather enough food to fuel its fast-paced metabolism. Even so, a hummer spends only an estimated 20 percent of its day foraging and takes the rest of the day off to relax.

Shake a tail feather
At the end of a dramatic dive, a male hummer spreads its tail feathers to create a chirpy song that impresses females.

Feathers
The hummingbird has no inside layer of downy feathers but boasts denser-than-usual coverage of more than 900 feathers. Even so, the lack of insulation is a stress when the temperature drops.

Feet
The hummingbird uses its tiny feet only for scratching and perching, not for walking or launching into flight.

Ears
With an ear on either side of its head, the hummingbird easily picks up the sounds of wing beats and vocalizations.

Brain power
At roughly 4.2 percent of its body weight, the hummingbird's brain is among the largest brain-to-body weight ratios of any bird.

Bill
Made from keratin, like our fingernails, the hummer's bill comes in a variety of shapes and lengths. All species use it to probe flower blossoms for nectar and sometimes as a weapon against competitors.

Eyes
The big eyes of a hummingbird are packed with cells that contain light-sensitive pigments. The hummer is quickly able to focus and detect detail.

Tongue pump
High-speed photography suggests that the hummer's tongue may act like a tiny elastic pump that is activated upon contact with nectar.

Length and weight
The rufous hummingbird is 3½ to 3⅞ inches (9–10 cm) long and weighs from 3 to 4.5 grams.

INCREDIBLE JOURNEY
The ruby-throated hummingbird, seen below, is the only hummingbird to enjoy family life in the eastern United States and eastern Canada. Each spring, this popular hummer doubles its body weight before joining millions of songbirds as they fly some 500 miles (800 km) across the Gulf of Mexico. Refueling on spring flower nectar in the southern United States, they fly on to their summer homes.

NATURAL TALENTS

In a big, competitive world, it is vital to have as much data as possible about sources of food, potential mates and enemies. With no olfactory nerves in its nasal cavities, the hummingbird doesn't have a sense of smell, but it is well equipped with its other senses: sight, hearing, taste and touch.

Perhaps the most critical sense for the hummingbird is sight. On the wing, the hummer counts on its ability to visually pinpoint its food targets. Its large, globular eyes, like those of a bird of prey, are highly placed on the sides of its head. In flight, the eyes are kept moist by a transparent third eyelid that also keeps out foreign objects.

When glancing to the side, the hummer sees with only one eye but has binocular vision when looking straight ahead. Packed with cells that contain light-sensitive pigments, its eyes can detect subtle details in the dark, dense understory of the rainforest and can see bright colors, which is critical when you make your living by identifying nectar-rich blossoms. Since the male hummingbird is often much more dramatically outfitted than the female, color recognition also plays a role in mating.

Recent research has revealed surprising news about the hummer's sense of taste. The hummingbird does not have a sweet-taste receptor, which raises

EYES ON THE WORLD
One of the nine "brilliants," the medium-sized Gould's jewelfront is found in tropical and equatorial South America, where it feeds on the nectar of flowering shrubs and scoops up flying insects. Under pressure from deforestation in its range, it has managed to adapt to changing habitats.

TOOLS OF THE TRADE
The color of a hummingbird's feathers is dependent on the angle of the light striking its plumage. This fiery-throated hummingbird shows off a rainbow of hues. The Costa's hummingbird, below, hovers for a sweet drink of nectar.

the question: How does a bird with a major sweet tooth identify its favorite food? Scientists now believe that over time, the hummer may have repurposed the receptor that recognizes meaty and savory flavors to appreciate nectar.

And while we once thought that capillary action allowed the hummingbird to wick up flower nectar with its grooved tongue, some researchers now believe that this bird's complex tongue works like a little pump, expanding and collapsing as it drives nectar into the tongue grooves.

Like other birds, the hummingbird relies on its hearing to suss out threats and to communicate with its fellows, making short and long songs and calls that may be high-pitched, piercing or soft and rhythmic.

To keep its gorgeous feathers healthy, the hummer preens itself with its beak, removing dirt and parasites and distributing oil from a gland on the base of its tail. It uses its tiny claws to get at hard-to-reach spots and to clean its beak.

SMELL

With no sense of smell, the hummer is drawn to flowers by their bright colors, not their scent.

TASTE

The hummer loves a sweet drink of nectar, but it also enjoys flying insects snatched from the air with its steel-trap beak.

SIGHT

With its big eyes, the hummer has excellent vision. It sees more hues than humans, including ultraviolet colors.

TOUCH

For the hummer, including this green-crowned brilliant, preening its feathers to keep them healthy and clean is a top priority.

HEARING

A hummer is able to detect and interpret small changes in pitch and tone better than most humans.

PLANNED PARENTHOOD

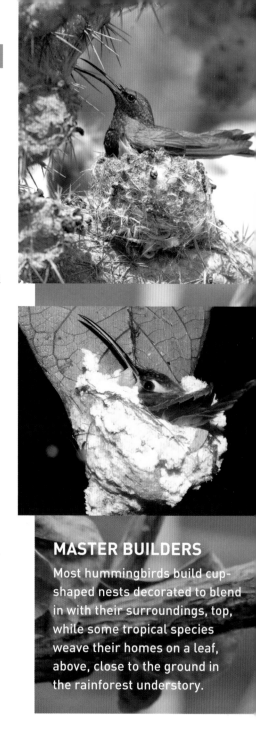

The female hummingbird is the definition of independent. Long before she finds a male partner, this forward-thinking mother-to-be is zipping around the neighborhood preparing a home for her offspring. Energetic and efficient, the female knows this is a responsibility she'll assume all on her own.

In choosing a nesting site, the female doesn't leave much to chance. In repeat visits, she test-drives tree twigs, branches or leaves to make sure they're strong enough to hold the weight of a nest and family. Sites might also include a rocky ledge, a clay riverbank, the underside of a bridge or the rafters of a barn. The far-ranging Anna's hummingbird may build her nest on a ready-made foundation, such as on the top of a pinecone. A desert-loving Costa's hummer may construct hers on a cactus plant in sunny Arizona.

The architectural style of a hummingbird nest can vary, but it must provide the basics for the whole family: warmth, shelter and security. The most common design is an open cup-shaped nest that is just large enough to hold the mother, two white, jelly-bean-sized eggs and the future nestlings. Building materials are whatever is close at hand—plant down, seeds and mosses, with a soft lining of feathers or hair. Hummingbirds that live near humans may snatch up bits of yarn and string. The female camouflages the nest by

MASTER BUILDERS
Most hummingbirds build cup-shaped nests decorated to blend in with their surroundings, top, while some tropical species weave their homes on a leaf, above, close to the ground in the rainforest understory.

A TINY, PERFECT HOME

The world's smallest birds build the smallest nests. Nest building can take a female anywhere from a day or two to two weeks. The Costa's hummingbird, right, has secured her little nest in the crotch of a slim tree limb.

TWO'S COMPANY

A hummingbird typically lays two eggs, though not always on the same day. The female delays incubating the first egg until the second egg appears, so the eggs hatch at the same time.

DELIVERY GUARANTEED

A female green violetear spends most of her time and energy searching for food for her young, bringing home a tasty regurgitated meal of nectar and tiny insects for her hungry offspring every 25 to 30 minutes.

weaving leaves, lichens and strips of bark to the outer surface, working carefully to conceal it from would-be predators. But the most important material is spiderweb silk, one of nature's strongest materials. A master seamstress, the female binds the nest together with sticky, barely visible pieces of silk, using nature's Krazy Glue to secure the nest to its foundation as well.

Tropical residents like the hermits construct nests that hang on the tip of a drooping broad palm, banana or heliconia leaf. On the wing and using her needlelike bill, the female weaves a cone-shaped cocoon of plant fibers that looks like a tiny sleeping bag. To make sure the nest hangs properly, she may collect little lumps of clay or pebbles with her beak and weave them into the nest.

Females are so efficient in their nest-building and family-rearing skills that some are able to produce two broods in one season,

depending on the availability of food and the weather. Sometimes, a female may be off building her second home before her first family has even left the nest.

Once her nest is ready, the female is free to search for the best mate she can find. In the hummingbird world, that's the male with the energy and strength to guard a plentiful garden of nectar-rich flowers. With the help of his often brilliant colors, he must prove those abilities by dazzling the female with the most impressive courtship displays. In the short, hardworking life of the female hummingbird, every choice counts.

EMPTY NEST SYNDROME

A rufous hummingbird nestling snuggles inside a cozy cup nest that is roughly one inch (2.5 cm) deep and two inches (5 cm) wide. After 18 to 28 days of tender loving care, this young bird will be ready to go off on its own. Its mother may have already started a new nest for her next family.

FLIGHTS OF FANCY

From its physical characteristics and mind-boggling metabolic measurements to its dazzling beauty, this family of birds stands out like few others. Yet among the long list of the hummingbird's talents, perhaps the most elaborate and mesmerizing is flight. With a rare combination of energy, intensity, grace and ferocity, the hummingbird is a true aerial performer.

Courtship is a fascinating behavior in the world of birds, but the male hummingbird takes this springtime ritual to a whole new level. As we know, the male plays no part in nest building or rearing its young, but he does throw a lot into his ambition to be a father. With elaborate flying displays,

brilliant plumage and song, the male hummingbird brings a trifecta of talents to the dating game.

Some males, perhaps spurred on by the challenge of competition, gather at a communal ground known as a lek. Lekking is especially popular among the group of tropical and subtropical hummingbirds known as the hermits. Garbed in mostly muted colors, the male hermit fans his tail feathers and shows off the brightly colored interior of his mouth to get a female's attention. Participants can range from a couple of birds to 20 or more, and the female has a chance to compare and contrast before picking a mate.

Other hummers prefer to work solo. A male Anna's hum-

FIGHT CLUB
Denizens of the Andes, a pair of booted racket-tail hummingbirds, top, display their unusual tail feathers as they face off, perhaps in a battle for food. Note the puffy white "boots" around their legs. Above: Flaring its violet ear feathers and spreading its tail feathers, this brown violetear is the definition of aerial self-confidence.

HE'S ALL THAT

This tufted coquette is extravagantly decked out in plumage fit for a king. Well under three inches long (7.5 cm) and less than three grams in weight, the coquette is one of the smaller hummers. But with his head crest on full alert, he's not letting size mess up his chances for romance.

mingbird hits 60 miles per hour (100 km/h) in a powerful dive that concludes with an extravagant spreading of his tail feathers and a loud chirping sound. Other males employ a "shuttle flight," flying a series of short flights a mere foot away from the female. Sometimes a buzzing vocalization is included. The male Allen's hummingbird leads up to his dive with a "pendulum display," swooping back and forth in front of his intended.

Whether puffing up his crest or neck feathers, singing at the top of his lungs for hours, day after day, or producing loud noises with his feathers, the male hummer is willing to spend a lot of time and energy to pass on his genes.

ONE FOR THE ROAD

As part of his courtship display, the male ruby-throated hummingbird, right, makes a tik-tik tik-tik tik-tik sound with his wings. Once the female, left, succumbs to his charms, he'll be on his way.

NECTAR HUNTERS

The sheer diversity of the New World's hummingbird family is well matched by an equally diverse number of flowering plants, and this goes a long way to explaining the success of each. Nectar-producing flowers are found in habitats ranging from tropical rainforests and temperate forests to dry deserts and chilly alpine zones, and the hummingbird is always close at hand. In this mutually beneficial system, the hummer receives a reward of nectar while dutifully picking up pollen on its beak and depositing it on a nearby plant. Voilà! The plant's genes carry on, and the hummer lives to feed another day.

There's more. Hummingbirds and plants have evolved traits to make one another's lives simpler. Some hummer beaks are long (the length of the sword-billed hummer's is four inches/10 cm), ideal for feeding on passionflowers. Some bills are short and straight (the shortest, at ½ inch/1.3 cm, belongs to the purple-backed thornbill), all the better for feeding at a wide variety of flowers with an open face. Other beaks are long and curved to fit into unusually shaped flowers.

The flower goes one better, making sure its pollen-laden stamens are perfectly positioned within the blossom to ensure a pollen takeaway for a particular hummer species. And because its partner in crime is designed to hover while feeding, the plant can do away with landing surfaces that might make it appealing to other birds and flying insects.

The size and shape of the bill also determine a hummingbird's approach to feeding. Long-billed hermits specialize in the tubular flowers of the tropical forest, which are spread across a wide area. These birds have devised a feeding strategy called traplining, in which they regularly follow a specific route to visit nectar-rich flowers.

Other hummingbirds are highly territorial, ferociously defending a patch of flowering plants against any intruders. Predictably, males like to commandeer the best territories, downsizing females to low-rent districts where the nectar isn't quite so plentiful. If you've ever watched a male ruby-throated hummer relentlessly drive another hummingbird from a feeder, you know just what we're talking about.

SPECIAL ACCESS

We may not know why this hermit's color is muted rather than bright, but we do know why its bill is long and curved: Hummingbird beaks and flowering plants have evolved together for their mutual success.

BILL PLEASE

With its down-curved beak, a violet sabrewing, top, feeds on nectar from a plant in the rainforest understory. The sword-billed hummingbird, above, has the longest beak in the world relative to its body size. All hummers round out their diet with protein by eating insects.